Jezebel Rising.

Satan's secret weapon against Hebrew Israelite men.....

By

Elderyoungman-Brother DL Williams

YHWH's Light

www.YHWHsLight.com

Table of Contents.

Revelation 2:18-29

King James Version (KJV)

18 And unto the angel of the church in Thyatira write; These things saith the Son of YHWH, who hath his eyes like unto a flame of fire, and his feet are like fine brass;

19 I know thy works, and charity, and service, and faith, and thy patience, and thy works; and the last to be more than the first.

20 Notwithstanding I have a few things against thee, because thou sufferest that woman Jezebel, which calleth herself a prophetess, to teach and to seduce my servants to commit fornication, and to eat things sacrificed unto idols.

21 And I gave her space to repent of her fornication; and she repented not.

22 Behold, I will cast her into a bed, and them that commit adultery with her into great tribulation, except they repent of their deeds.

23 And I will kill her children with death; and all the churches shall know that I am he which searcheth the reins and hearts: and I will give unto every one of you according to your works.

24 But unto you I say, and unto the rest in Thyatira, as many as have not this doctrine, and which have not known the depths of Satan, as they speak; I will put upon you none other burden.

25 But that which ye have already hold fast till I come.

26 And he that overcometh, and keepeth my works unto the end, to him will I give power over the nations:

27 And he shall rule them with a rod of iron; as the vessels of a potter shall they be broken to shivers: even as I received of my Father.

28 And I will give him the morning star.

29 He that hath an ear, let him hear what the Spirit saith unto the churches.

1. Introduction.

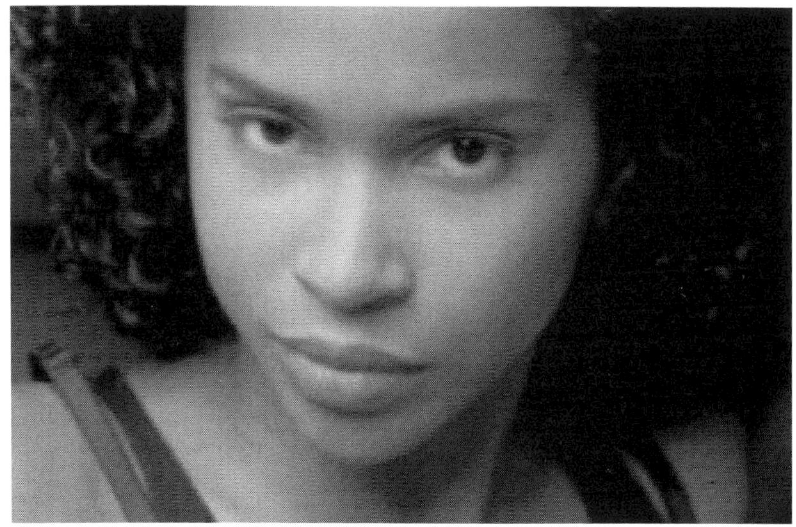

What is this spirit and where did it come from?

Welcome to "Jezebel Rising" and thank you for your support! I have to ask, how did we end up here? How has shameless twerking become both popular and mainstream? Why is Homosexuality so widely accepted in Christian Black (Hebrew) women? Where are the men and the preachers? Why aren't the men speaking out against this obvious rot in our society? The short answer to this question is that "Jezebel" has "Risen". This spirit didn't just "Happen" to seduce Ahab, wipe out and persecute the Prophets of our Father and bring Israel to only 7000 men unaffected by her witchcraft. Not even close! This spirit is high in Satan's hierarchy and very powerful. It's time is now, the end or the age of Aquarius. Know your enemy brothers and sisters.......

This writing will be (I hope) a valuable tool in understanding our times and also gaining some insight into what is going on with today's woman. We are going to walk through the spiritual battle being fought by women who strive to be in order and what is in control of those many women who have come to the place where the "Word" of the Holy Scriptures has become debatable. Indeed, there has been a change to the minds of our women and also a change in us brothers, where we don't care for the Father's order and even if we do, we don't fight to see the order kept.

There is a reason that the Glorified MessiYah singles out one of the seven churches of Asia Minor about the spirit of Jezebel. It is our responsibility to be sensitive to and to stand against this spirit. To do that, you have to understand who Jezebel was in the flesh. We have to understand how she was raised and the land that she comes from. We have to know what spirits possessed her. We also have to know the footprint of this demon and finally, we must have a clear understanding of how to be victorious over this demon.

By the end of this book, you will have a new understanding of what you see every day.

Shalom and thank you again for your support!

Elderyoungman.....

Brother DL Williams................

2. Who Was Jezebel (in the flesh)?

1 Kings 16:30-31

[30] *And Ahab the son of Omri did evil in the sight of the LORD above all that were before him.*

[31] *And it came to pass, as if it had been a light thing for him to walk in the sins of Jeroboam the son of Nebat, that he took to wife Jezebel the daughter of Ethbaal king of the Zidonians, and went and served Baal, and worshipped him.*

We all know the KJV description of Jezebel, from the approved 66 books of the canon. Jezebel was the Babylonian princess married by Israel's king, Ahab, during the time and ministry of EliYah (Elijah) the prophet. She stands out among those who influenced the kings of Father YHWH's people in that her overt influence, coupled with Ahab's passive (punk) nature caused a genocide amongst the faithful prophets of the Most High. Israel at the time of EliYah's encounter with the prophets of Baal was reduced to only 7000 faithful men.

That's the common knowledge or what I'd like to call the prettied version. What was really going on is much more similar to what you see in today's world. Jezebel was able to "Manipulate" Ahab into allowing all of these unholy things to go on. How did she do this? She put that "Thang" on Ahab and cracked him out sexually. This by no means excuses Ahab from his role in what happened in our homeland, but is only the "How". Ahab's weakness was ultimately the cause of death for many of his own countrymen. Make a note leaders! More than just the physical superiority that Jezebel exerted over Ahab, you have to understand that this "Princess" lived her life and was trained to be an open vessel for fallen angelic and demonic spirits. When Jezebel physically "put it on" Ahab, those spirits that had walked and talked with her all her life, were imparted to Ahab and took possession of him.

Yes, Jezebel was a sister….

Jezebel was the daughter of a man named Ethbaal, king of Tyre in Phoenicia. Who were the Phoenicians? The Phoenicians were described as the mariners or inhabitants of the coasts of the fertile crescent. These were the descendents of the Canaanites. For those who understand the origins of ancient paganism, there is really no more to be said. She was raised by a high priest of Baal and was a priestess of Asherah. The worship associated with these two fallen deities involves child sacrifice and overt sexual immorality. What you read in the canon, without supplemental study does not in any way provide a full description of what the kingdom of Israel became under Ahab and Jezebel. The places of worship became literal whore-houses, where women opened themselves up not only to the phallic worship of the priests of Baal, but to every demon spirit they communed with. This resulted in possession and apostasy not seen in the holy land up until this point. The overt and uncontrolled sexual immorality resulted in unwanted children. These children became sacrifices to the fallen angels and Baal. This filth filled the land and was virtually unopposed until the ministry of EliYah the prophet.

Through manipulation of Ahab, Jezebel was able to wage war on the Father's chosen nation from the inside. From the bedroom, Jezebel was able to kill almost all of the faithful prophets of YHWH. She was able to purge and alter the whole structure of worship and the true representation of our Father here on the earth.

From a more broad perspective and also in the over all war being waged between man's redemption and Satan's attempts to stop man's redemption, it is very clear that Jezebel was intended to be the nail in the coffin of YHWH's plan to redeem His creation. Satan's war with Adam and then the children of Adam, the corruption of Nimrod and the empowering of Babylon in the earth, all of these things were intended to corrupt and disrupt the coming of our MessiYah, Yahshua. The first and second books of the kings follow the seed of sin, sown in Adam, through the house of King David. One of the punishments that our Father placed on King David was that the kingdom would be split, but not in his time, but the time of his son, Solomon. King Solomon's life at the end was a foreshadowing of what would happen in the life of Ahab. Hebrew Israelite men were commanded by our Father not to take heathen women for wives and this was so that the generations of children would not be influenced by the heathen traditions of such wives. The mother of Solomon's heir, Rehoboam was such a woman. Naamah, wife of King Solomon, was an Ammonite woman. The Ammonites were one of the peoples born of Lot and his daughters, who got him drunk and slept with him. In other words, the mothers of these peoples had the influences of being raise in Sodom and Gomorrah. The Ammonites took on the worship of Moloch, the owl god, which traces itself back to Baal and Nimrod. When the kingdom split under Rehoboam, the new northern kingdom anointed a man named Jeroboam as their king. Jeroboam immediately took the kingdom into the direction of Baal and Asherah worship. This decision haunted all of the kings of the northern kingdom and contributed to the spiritual separation (death) of these tribes of YHWH's chosen people. This decision also made what was ultimately sold to the kingdom by Jezebel common.

Many wars between the Hebrew and heathen nations were fought. Whether they were described as the Japhethites, Babylonians, Canaanites, what have you, but none were as effective as the appeal of voluntary corruption by sin. Jezebel was successful in her persuasion of Ahab and the people because she gave them what they wanted. The introduction of her overt whoredom and the acceptance of this whoredom by the leadership gave the people exactly the excuse they needed to fall into apostasy.

So, again, I ask "Who was Jezebel in the flesh"? She was the embodiment of overt sexual perversion's influence over what we would call leadership in the things of the Most High. By positioning herself in what we would call the church, she was able to emasculate and spiritually divide the multitudes of men, who could ultimately have become mighty in the kingdom of YHWH Most High. More than this, she is the poster child of unsubmission AND unrepented pride. Her mission was to manipulate or destroy men of power, in the Kingdom of YHWH.

Discerning this spirit will require spiritual sensitivity and the death of the flesh...

Now that we know the "Person" of Jezebel, we also need to know the force necessary to balance her influence. The person of Jezebel pressed her influence in both the spiritual and physical worlds, similar to the complete fall of man. The Spiritual fall happened in the garden. The Physical, in the realm of the corruption from Genesis 6 and the Book of Enoch, with the angels having sex with the daughters of men. Jezebel's corruption of the worship caused a spiritual rot in the nation of Israel. This "Rot" caused Ahab to be known as the Israelite king that did evil in the sight of our Father and provoked our Father, more so than any other before him. That's serious!

1 Kings 16:33

33 And Ahab made a grove; and Ahab did more to provoke the Most High of Israel to anger than all the kings of Israel that were before him.

This spiritual rot manifested itself into the physical world as those faithful to the Most High were persecuted and killed throughout the Holy Land, kind of like those who now oppose homosexuality in public. Like that time, people faithful to our Father had to work in secret to resist those wicked people in leadership. Obadiah, Ahab's governor was such a person.

1 Kings 18:4

3 And Ahab called Obadiah, which was the governor of his house. (Now Obadiah feared the FATHER greatly:

4 For it was so, when Jezebel cut off the prophets of the MOST HIGH, that Obadiah took an hundred prophets, and hid them by fifty in a cave, and fed them with bread and water.)

Spiritually, the influence of Jezebel was directly confronted by EliYah. The ultimate show down between he and the prophets of Baal caused a revival and spiritual conversion for the nation. The Father showed the impotence of Baal to His people and caused the satanic church to be overthrown. But the "Physical" person of Jezebel required a different sort all together. This "Sort" took the form of King Jehu.

NEVER remove your helmet or your armor...and if you lose the sword, you'll die...

The movie character that I think is most reminiscent of King Jehu is the character DREDD. As Jehu approached, Jezebel pulled together all of her feminine witchcraft and presented herself in the window. The character DREDD is never seen without his helmet, armor or weapon and that is ultimately the fact that every man that is called to battle Jezebel should take note of. If King Jehu was swayed by what was placed up in the window, the feminine witchcraft of Jezebel would have consumed him. In other writings, I have described King Jehu as "Murderous" and that description is not without warrant. As ruthless and calculating as Jezebel proved to be throughout her time as Israel's queen, King Jehu matched, stroke for stroke, Jezebel's intensity. 2 Kings 9-10 outlines the literal bloodbath that King Jehu inflicted upon Ahab's house, Judah's King that aligned himself with Ahab's house, Jezebel and the servants of Baal in the land. This literally blood-thirsty, yet obedient spirit within Jehu was diametrically opposite of the spirit in Ahab. The level of violence outlined in these two chapters of 2 Kings is a wake-up call for any man that has the courage to oppose Jezebel in this time. The person of Jezebel is really nothing in comparison to the spirit that possessed her. This spirit is ancient and is heavily influenced by this world's first female demon. But we will get on to that when we talk about who Jezebel "IS" today.

3. The ground that grew Jezebel....

As mentioned previously, Jezebel was born and raised in the Phoenician, Babylonian city of Tyre. Tyre was specifically sited in the bible on numerous occasions, but the citation most indicative of who Jezebel became is located in the 28th chapter of Ezekiel. In this chapter of scripture, the judgment of YHWH is being pronounced against the "Prince" of Tyre.

Ezekiel 28

2 *Son of man, say unto the prince of Tyrus, Thus saith the Most High; Because thine heart is lifted up, and thou hast said, I am a god, I sit in the seat of the Highest, in the midst of the seas; yet thou art a man, and not the Highest, though thou set thine heart as the heart of the Most High:*

3 *Behold, thou art wiser than Daniel; there is no secret that they can hide from thee:*

By the 12th verse, it becomes very apparent that the prophet is not only being instructed to preach to the man, but the spirit that resided in the man. The conversation turns to addressing the spirit of Satan himself, who is obviously in possession of and manipulating the person of the prince. Satan is identified as the "King" of Tyre.

Ezekiel 28

12 Son of man, take up a lamentation upon the king of Tyrus, and say unto him, Thus saith the the Most High; Thou sealest up the sum, full of wisdom, and perfect in beauty.

13 Thou hast been in Eden the garden of YHWH; every precious stone was thy covering, the sardius, topaz, and the diamond, the beryl, the onyx, and the jasper, the sapphire, the emerald, and the carbuncle, and gold: the workmanship of thy tabrets and of thy pipes was prepared in thee in the day that thou wast created.

Satan in his spirit form is the King of Tyre. He has been the spirit behind every anti-MessiYah that has walked to earth, from Nimrod, to Pharaoh, to Alexander, to Hitler and on and on. The city of Tyre's wealth is characteristic of where this fallen angel sets up his seat. Tyre was a major port city and center of commerce in the ancient world. Satan is known for setting up his seat in opulence and splendor, which for that time, was characteristic of Tyre. Tyre traded in the goods of the world and was famous for purple dyes used to dye the robes of the nobility.

As pointed out previously, the Phoenicians were descendents of the Canaanites and worshippers of Baal and Asherah. We hear that term so much that I think it cheapens what that actually means. The worship of the Canaanites, ancient paganism, is actually derived from the witchcraft of the fallen angels, from the days of Noah. Again, I don't think the words do justice to just how deep and dark this practice actually is. This witchcraft, revisited by Nimrod after the flood and resulting in the Rephiam (giants) in the land of Canaan at the time of the Exodus, was outright abomination against the Word of our Father. It is the pre-flood worship of the fallen angels, that brought the flood upon the world. It violates the commandment given to Noah after the flood regarding seed time and harvest.

This "Witchcraft" was structured on the creation of Idols and the direction of worship to those idols. Idols are described in the scriptures as the "Teraphim". These idols were the basis for divination and ancestor worship. The Teraphim was usually the head of a person's first born child. This is where the small skulls common to Halloween originate from. The Egyptians used a form of child sacrifice where instead of placing the head of a child on an alter inside of the home, the whole body of the first born child was built into the wall of a person's home. In short, the fallen angels led men to regard worthless, that which no man or angel can create. Life itself.

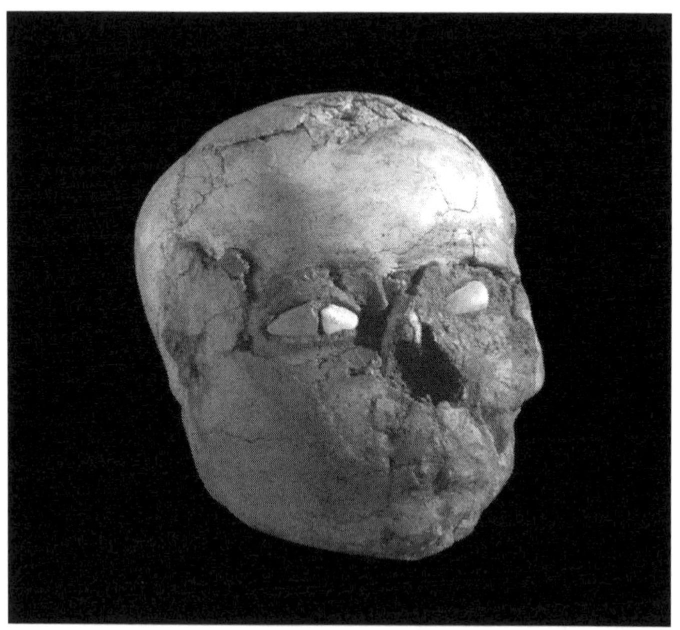

A "Teraphim" idol was usually the head of ones first born child.

The wasting of life through the blood has been an abomination since Cain took the first life (his brother's, Abel) and spilled blood on the earth for the first time. Canaan, Phoenicia, Babylon, Egypt, Assyria and all of the empires of the ancient world took part in this abominable form of worship. Tyre was one of the major centers of pagan worship. It was in this setting, Jezebel was trained with the ultimate goal of destroying the proper worship of YHWH Most High.

Through the overt sacrifice of life, people were able to make contact with the dead or cause the fallen angels to perform signs and favors. This was the reason that Hebrew and heathen kings immolated (burned) their children on alters to "other gods" or fallen angels. This worship and also the mingling of angelic DNA (Genesis 6) with the seed of man were the reasons that the land of Canaan was accursed and full of giants. This is also the reason that the Father's commands during the time of the Exodus were so absolute. Destroy them, their children, their cattle and possessions. Our ancestors were to leave nothing, because these things were dedicated to fallen angels and demon spirits. The Canaanites used magic, demonology, blood sacrifices and the ritual drinking of blood in their every day worship.

Acts of ritual sexual relations, bestiality and homosexuality all originated in the witchcraft of the fallen angels and were parts of Canaanite worship as it distorted and violated the original designs of Father YHWH. The concept of the painted or tattooed woman originates in this form of worship, where the women painted themselves to gain the attention of the temple priests. These priests would then select them for sexual worship. Again, this is where Jezebel was born and raised. This is where she learned the things she brought into the kingdom of Israel. She was literally bred and educated to oppose the ways and will of our Father.

The worship of feminine pagan deity always involved ritual sexual relations.

All of the practices, witchcraft and abominations outlined as a part of Jezebel's upbringing trace themselves back the tower of Babel and Nimrod. Nimrod himself "IS" Baal. His queen, Semiramis, who we will be discussing at length in the next chapter, "IS" Asherah. Nimrod rose to power and led the descendents of Noah into these pagan religious practices. He subjugated peoples with sorcery and technology others did not have. Just as the prince of Tyre was possessed of Satan, Nimrod was also. As the first post flood emperor, he and his queen set up financial, military and religious rule and set themselves up as the objects of worship. Many idols were set up and through these idols, fallen angels and demons received worship from man. This is the rebellion that the scriptures describe when talking about Nimrod's leadership of the people. This pagan, satanic religion has been with us since it was re-established by Nimrod and has not really changed much between that time and now. Jezebel's time in this world was dedicated to the worship of Nimrod and his queen, via the Babylonian Mystery religion, which is the basis for all pagan religions.

Leta the first queen of sparta had sex with Zeus in the form of a goose.

In understanding the prevailing climate in Tyre at the time, we can get a pretty clear picture of how truly wicked this Jezebel was. Seeing a child burned or butchered was nothing to her and as the daughter of Ethbaal and a priestess herself, she was constantly exposed to and participating in these abominable practices. Having all kinds of sex and sexual partners, male or female, was nothing to her. Sexual relations with animals, drug induced altered states, murder, sacrifice, adultery, you name it, she'd done it as a part of her upbringing under Ethbaal and her position as a priestess. Even more than this, serving and channeling demons and fallen angels, and how to do these things, would be something that Jezebel had been exposed to and worked with all of her life.

Ritual sexual immorality has been with us since antiquity.

What we have heard of in the later empires of the Greeks and Romans are just indicators of what went on in places like Tyre, Sodom and Egypt. Ultimately, the world has not changed that much, in that pagan Satanism still rules this world.

1 John 5:19
King James Version (KJV)

19 And we know that we are of Father YHWH, and the whole world lieth in wickedness.

It was in this way that the children of Israel were corrupted or spoiled as the scriptures say, during their time in Egypt. These habits were described as the "Stench" of Egypt. These spirits followed them and not 40 days without Moshe's supervision, the children immediately went back to the way of Baal worship and abomination. The calf was Nimrod and the Hebrews, our people, were having an orgy. Make a note.

4. Who IS Jezebel (the Demon that drives her)?

The Original Female Demon.

The first thing we have to understand about the chief demon (because there was more than one) that drove Jezebel during her life, we have to look back to way before her time. The characteristics of Jezebel, the hate, the violence, the whoredom, the murderous nature, the self centeredness, all of these things have shown up in the lives of other women figures in the scriptures and history. The book of Revelation identifies this "Spirit" as Jezebel because her life and the effects of this spirit against Father YHWH's chosen people is so well documented. An entire church is reprimanded by our MessiYah in His glorified form, because they walked in the way of Ahab and allowed the spirit of Jezebel to run wild.

Revelation 2

[20] Notwithstanding I have a few things against thee, because thou sufferest that woman Jezebel, which calleth herself a prophetess, to teach and to seduce my servants to commit fornication, and to eat things sacrificed unto idols.

[21] And I gave her space to repent of her fornication; and she repented not.

[22] Behold, I will cast her into a bed, and them that commit adultery with her into great tribulation, except they repent of their deeds.

[23] And I will kill her children with death; and all the churches shall know that I am he which searcheth the reins and hearts: and I will give unto every one of you according to your works.

[24] But unto you I say, and unto the rest in Thyatira, as many as have not this doctrine, and which have not known the depths of Satan, as they speak; I will put upon you none other burden.

This is the "Spirit" of Jezebel, not the literal person of Jezebel. This spirit existed well before Jezebel's life. To truly understand the dysfunctional depths of the this demon, we have to look at the life of the first queen of Babylon, Sammu-ramat or Semiramis.

If Nimrod was the father of all pagan religions, his wife, Sammu-ramat, was undoubtedly the mother. The deities formed at the tower of Babel, by way of the Babylonian Mystery religion were structured on the very persons of Nimrod, Semiramis and Tammuz.

This "Mother" deity has gone from empire to empire…

Nimrod was described in the Bible as a "Mighty Hunter of Men", which is clarified to mean that he was seducer and controller of the minds of men. This is significant because each iteration of what we call the "Sun God" has its basis in Nimrod's apostasy. His seduction caused man to worship man, in this case, Nimrod himself. He became Baal and originated the Baal worship that characterized the "Way of Jeroboam" that plagued the nation of Israel throughout its existence. Semiramis "IS" the consort to Baal or the pagan goddess Ashtoreth (Yes, the same one Jezebel worshipped). She was also called Ishtar in India, Juno in Rome, Isis in Egypt, Hera in Greece…basically any queen deity worshipped in the world, has its basis in the first queen of Babylon.

Mystery Babylon Tradition: Dying eggs in the blood of sacrificed infants on the altar to Easter (Ishtar) at sun-rise services for the pagan sun gods!

When the American Church repents of celebrating Easter, our prayers against Abortion will finally be answered! Until then, don't bother praying against Abortion until you come out of Mystery Babylon the Great the Mother of all Harlots! (Revelation 18:4)

Easter Eggs are actually derived from what the pagans called "Ishtar" eggs and the colors of these eggs were always red. The reason for this is the blood of the infants used to create teraphims were used to paint the eggs. Teraphims (big word) are the "Idols" that scripture refers to. The "Mother" goddess set up by Constantine, the venerated, deified virgin Mary is nothing more than another reference to the "Queen of Heaven" or Semiramis. The key to Nimrod's ability to rule his kingdom was to cause people's worship (love, material & actions) to be directed to him. His symbol was the sun while Semiramis' was the moon. Satan manipulated his ambitions to cause him to cause others, to take their eyes off of Father YHWH. Semiramis, before meeting Nimrod, was a harlot and a brothel house madamme. After becoming queen and being named the moon goddess, the Queen of Heaven, etc, she became pregnant illegitimately. Fearing the wrath of her king, she had Nimrod killed and took the throne.

When she gave birth to her child, she names him Tammuz and declared that he was Nimrod reincarnated (Some serious Jerry Springer type madness). As Tammuz (Ezekiel 8:14) grew to manhood, the spirit that possessed Semiramis caused her to attempt to kill her own child, because he was a man of power, which this demon cannot stand. The worship of Baal and Ashtoreth called for child sacrifice, ritual prostitution and sexual immorality and in some extreme cases, cannibalism. The prophet Ezekiel mentions Tammuz directly when describing Israel's love of Baal worship.

Though Semiramis is less well known than Jezebel, it is very apparent that Jezebel channeled the same demonic spirit and worshipped the "Queen of Heaven" who is Semiramis. Nimrod was not the weakling that Ahab was, so Semiramis had him killed according to one of the texts. This demon is drawn to power and will try to dominate all that it comes into contact with. It will cause its host to do ANYTHING to empower itself and dominate the lives of others. Outward manifestations take the form of relentless mental torment, resulting in depression and physical illness. This demon simply destroys weak men, their lives and anything attached to them. You see this demon's influence in the lives of other wicked women in the scriptures. The venom and doggedness that Delilah nagged Samson points its origins at a demonic influence. Herodias' rage with Yohannon (John) the Baptist, to the point of having him executed, has its roots in the same demonic influence. Potifar's wife was reduced to a demonic form of hatred when she was denied what she thought she wanted from Yohseph (Joseph), which also resulted in her attempting to have this man killed.

But, if a spirit possessed Jezebel, also Semiramis before her and this spirit showed up over and over again throughout scripture and is with us today, that can only mean that this spirit is bigger and stronger than just Jezebel, Semiramis or any of the others. This line of logic holds true and traces itself all the way back to garden of Eden. I've written on this before (Volume 1 of "This World's War on Fathers and Family-Our Women), but the study only seems to gain relevance to the lives we live today.

The first Female Demon....Adam's First Wife... Lilith....

Genesis 1:27:

"So The Father created man in his own image, in the image of YHWH created He ***him****; male and female created He them."—KJV*

So, in 1:27, our Father created "Man" in his own image, both male and female. Some translations even go so far as to say that the "Him" highlighted above should actually say "Them", suggesting that Father YHWH actually created "Both", one male (Adam) and one female (not Eve). You have to really pay close attention to the wording here. Our Father created a male and a "Female". To them He said "Go forth and be fruitful". But, in Genesis 2:7, Abba "Formed" the man from the dust of the ground.

Genesis 2:7

"And the Most High formed man of the dust of the ground, and breathed into his nostrils the breath of life; and man became a living soul."

So Father YHWH created "Man" in his own image, both male and female, but he "FORMED" man, not mankind or woman, of the dust of the ground. He then put the "Man" in the garden, alone. We know that the "Formed" man was alone because Father YHWH said it wasn't good for him to be that way (Gen 2:18). Then, in Genesis 2:22, Father takes the rib of the man (a part of his own body) and creates for him a

"Suitable" mate. Now I want you all to read these verses very carefully and see if you catch what jumped off of the page at me.

Genesis 2:21-23

21 *And the Most High caused a deep sleep to fall upon Adam, and he slept: and He took one of his ribs, and closed up the flesh instead thereof;*

22 *And the rib, which the MOST HIGH had taken from man, made He a woman, and brought her unto the man.*

23 *And Adam said, This is now bone of my bones, and flesh of my flesh: she shall be called Woman, because she was taken out of Man.*

Did you catch it? Adam's first wife was named Lilith. According the Book of Adam, the Alphabet of Bin Sira, the Hebrew Midrash, the Gilgamesh writings and many other ancient writings, Adam had more than one wife. Lilith was created at the same time as Adam but something happened to her before the second chapter. Before we get into what happened to Lilith and I explain to you why I am convinced that her spirit was the chief demon that drove Jezebel, Semiramis and the others, there is one critical thing to understand about the difference between Lilith and Eve. In the first chapter, Adam's wife was described as a "Female". Eve was created from the formed body of Adam (from his rib) and she was not called "Female", but a "Wo-Man" or a Man with a Womb. This fact is absolutely huge in understanding the current mental state of "Women". Eve is NOT "Female" according to the scriptures. A Female never came out of man. A "Woman" was created from man and her place was assigned by our Father. A woman is to be a help-meet to her husband and the husband is to rule over and cover the woman. I didn't make that up, it is the word of our Father. The temptation to rebel was initiated by Satan, but in some translations and as shown to us in some religious art, Adam and Eve were not alone in the garden with a serpent. Lilith is represented in the garden of Eden at the fall as a woman with a serpents body from the waist down.

Was "Lilith" actually the serpent Satan entered?

The story of Lilith is an interesting one. When the Father issued the first command to Adam and the "Female" image (Lilith) he told them to go forth, be fruitful and multiply. Lilith refused to submit to the man and refused to have sexual relations with Adam in a submissive position. She left Adam and fled away to the sea, where she met and had sexual relations with Eblis or Satan. She began to birth demon children. Adam petitioned Father YHWH to bring her back and our Father dispatched 3 angels who went to Lilith with the Father's commands. She refused and was cursed. She became a demon. As a punishment for her rebellion against our Father, the angels were to kill 300 of her demon children per day until the end of time. Lilith became a succubus, raping men in their sleep to steal their semen. Lilith also became the murderer of the children of Eve, particularly male children, because of the seed.

The Alphabet of Ben Sira on Lilith

After Father YHWH created Adam, who was alone, He said, 'It is not good for man to be alone' (Gen.2:18). He then created a woman for Adam, from the earth, as He had created Adam himself, and called her Lilith. Adam and Lilith began to fight. She said, 'I will not lie below,' and he said, 'I will not lie beneath you, but only on top. For you are fit only to be in the bottom position, while am to be in the superior one.' Lilith responded, 'We are equal to each other inasmuch as we were both created from the earth.' But they would not listen to one another. When Lilith saw this, she pronounced the Ineffable Name and flew away into the air. Adam stood in prayer before his Creator: 'Sovereign of the universe!' he said, 'the woman you gave me has run away.' At once, the Holy One, blessed be He, sent these three angles to bring her back. "Said the Holy One to Adam, 'If she agrees to come back, fine. If not she must permit one hundred of her children to die every day.' The angels left the Most High and pursued Lilith, whom they overtook in the midst of the sea, in the mighty waters wherein the Egyptians were destined to drown. They told her Abba's word, but she did not wish to return. The angels said, 'We shall drown you in the sea.'

"'Leave me!' she said. 'I was created only to cause sickness to infants. If the infant is male, I have dominion over him for eight days after his birth, and if female, for twenty days.' "When the angels heard Lilith's words, they insisted she go back. But she swore to them by the name of the living and eternal Sovereign: 'Whenever I see you or your names or your forms in an amulet, I will have no power over that infant.' She also agreed to have one hundred of her children die every day. Accordingly, every day one hundred demons perish, and for the same reason, we write the angels' names on the amulets of young children. When Lilith sees their names, she remembers her oath, and the child recovers."

Wikipedia on Lilith:

Main article: Alphabet of Ben Sira

The pseudepigraphic[51] 8th-10th centuries Alphabet of Ben Sira is considered to be the oldest form of the story of Lilith as Adam's first wife. Whether this particular tradition is older is not known. Scholars tend to date the Alphabet between the 8th and 10th centuries AD.

In the text an amulet is inscribed with the names of three angels (Senoy, Sansenoy, and Semangelof) and placed around the neck of newborn boys in order to protect them from the lilin until their circumcision.[52] The amulets used against Lilith that were thought to derive from this tradition are, in fact, dated as being much older.[53] The concept of Eve having a predecessor is not exclusive to the Alphabet, and is not a new concept, as it can be found in Genesis Rabbah. However, the idea that Lilith was the predecessor is exclusive to the Alphabet.

The idea in the text that Adam had a wife prior to Eve may have developed from an interpretation of the Book of Genesis and its dual creation accounts; while Genesis 2:22 describes God's creation of Eve from Adam's rib, an earlier passage, 1:27, already indicates that a woman had been made: "So God created man in his own image, in the image of God created he him; male and female created he them." The Alphabet text places Lilith's creation after God's words in Genesis 2:18 that "it is not good for man to be alone"; in this text God forms Lilith out of the clay from which he made Adam but she and Adam bicker. Lilith claims that since she and Adam were created in the same way they were equal and she refuses to submit to him:[54] The background and purpose of The Alphabet of Ben-Sira is unclear. It is a collection of stories about heroes of the Bible and Talmud, it may have been a collection of folk-tales, a refutation of Christian, Karaite, or other separatist movements; its content seems so offensive to contemporary Jews that it was even suggested that it could be an anti-Jewish satire,[55] although, in any case, the text was accepted by the Jewish mystics of medieval Germany.

The Alphabet of Ben-Sira is the earliest surviving source of the story, and the conception that Lilith was Adam's first wife became only widely known with the 17th century Lexicon Talmudicum of German scholar Johannes Buxtorf.

In this folk tradition that arose in the early Middle Ages Lilith, a dominant female demon, became identified with Asmodeus, King of Demons, as his queen.[56] Asmodeus was already well known by this time because of the legends about him in the Talmud. Thus, the merging of Lilith and Asmodeus was inevitable.[57] The second myth of Lilith grew to include legends about another world and by some accounts this other world existed side by side with this one,Yenne Velt is Yiddish for this described "Other World". In this case Asmodeus and Lilith were believed to procreate demonic offspring endlessly and spread chaos at every turn.[58] Many disasters were blamed on both of them, causing wine to turn into vinegar, men to be impotent, women unable to give birth, and it was Lilith who was blamed for the loss of infant life. The presence of Lilith and her cohorts were considered very real at this time.[citation needed]

Two primary characteristics are seen in these legends about Lilith: Lilith as the incarnation of lust, causing men to be led astray, and Lilith as a child-killing witch, who strangles helpless neonates. Although these two aspects of the Lilith legend seemed to have evolved separately, there is hardly a tale where she encompasses both roles.[58] But the aspect of the witch-like role that Lilith plays broadens her archetype of the destructive side of witchcraft. Such stories are commonly found among Jewish folklore.

The lullaby, songs sung over the beds of infant children, have their origins in the legend of the Lilith demon. Rebellion, vengeance and hatred of men became the trade mark of this demon. Now one can say that this is all just remote religious superstition, but the fact is that this demon is invoked more in our current society than it was even during the times of queens Jezebel or Semiramis. All trauma induced mind control in women seeks to create the idea that a man or a woman's proper place in relation to the man, is not needed. Today, women and girls are trained to be "Females" or equal to the man, not a "Women" and in the proper order of Father YHWH.

1 Corintians 11:7-12

7 For a man indeed ought not to cover his head, forasmuch as he is the image and glory of God: but the woman is the glory of the man.

8 For the man is not of the woman: but the woman of the man.

9 Neither was the man created for the woman; but the woman for the man.

10 For this cause ought the woman to have power on her head because of the angels.

11 Nevertheless neither is the man without the woman, neither the woman without the man, in the Lord.

12 For as the woman is of the man, even so is the man also by the woman; but all things of God.

This is done to create in the woman a spirit of destruction that hates order, is unrepentant and evil beyond the realm of reason. Lilith's rebellion was a foreshadowing of Eve's rebellion. Eve eventually repented of her rebellion, but only after she was shown that Satan had used her to destroy Adam. Eve was basically the first Jezebel, who led her husband to his destruction and damnation for the whole world, but repented of what she had done. Today, however, the rebellious wickedness of women is celebrated.

With this knowledge in place, one would think that today's woman would run to get back into the order of our Father... Right? Wrong! That would be too easy. Today, Lilith's rebellion is worshipped by feminists and lesbians. This outright rebellion against the order and will of our Father is now taught to young women and is passed off as strength and independence, while at its core, it is deeply satanic and outright witchcraft.

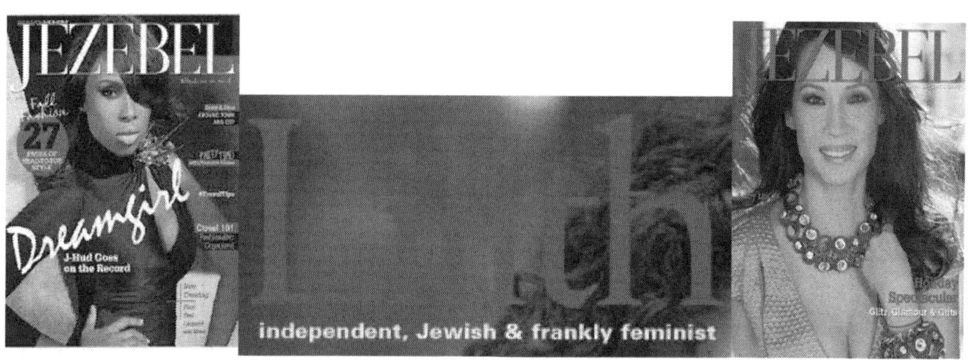

The "Mindset" is sold as stylish and strong.....

We allow it to be taught to our daughters at a young age and we wonder why our world is in chaos? While Jezebel rises, what are we men doing? Most males aren't men at all. We enjoy the fact that these women are whores and then are surprised when these same women can't cook or clean and then they try to teach the younger women to be the same whores while teaching our sons to be soft and woman-like. It's something to think about.

5. The Jezebel demon (Lilith) today...

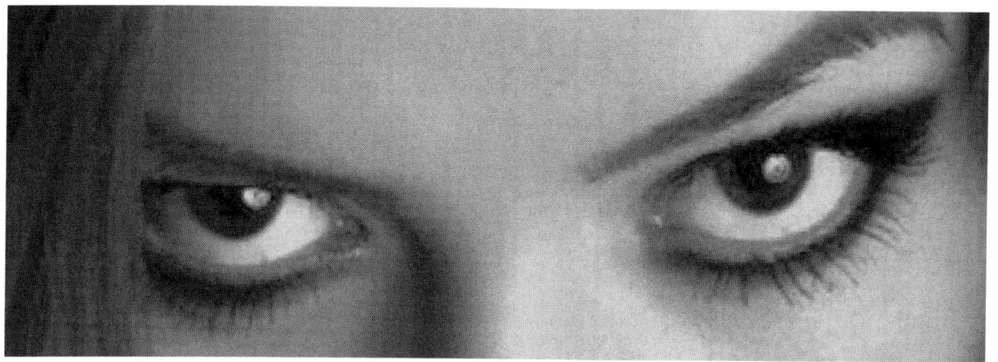

Proverbs 7:25-27

King James Version (KJV)

25 Let not thine heart decline to her ways, go not astray in her paths.

26 For she hath cast down many wounded: yea, many strong men have been slain by her.

27 Her house is the way to hell, going down to the chambers of death.

In today's world, the spirit of Jezebel has been commissioned to run rampant and it is doing just that. Satanism, rebellion and femininity have become synonymous in the minds of many and as was stated by the Satanist Anton Lavey in 1966, "Through the Female demon, Satan would rule the age of Aquarius". This demon was called "Babylon" by Satanist Alister Crawley and her wickedness is openly revered amongst those who are out of the natural order of our Father, YHWH Most High. In times passed, those who live openly in rebellion to the order of our Father were a shadowy group of rejects who practiced their lifestyles and witchcraft in secret. This has changed significantly in today's world and through women who act like "Females" and are out of order, Satanism has gone mainstream. Of course, the women don't rule in Satan's kingdom, but just as the Germanic Arians would send out Valkyries to bewitch men's minds, before a battle, so have a small group of Satanistic men used entertainment media, movies, schools, celebrities and the church (we will discuss this further in the next chapter) to promote outright Satanism without penalty or backlash. The things you see today in the media would literally be illegal to show on the air waves in generations passed.

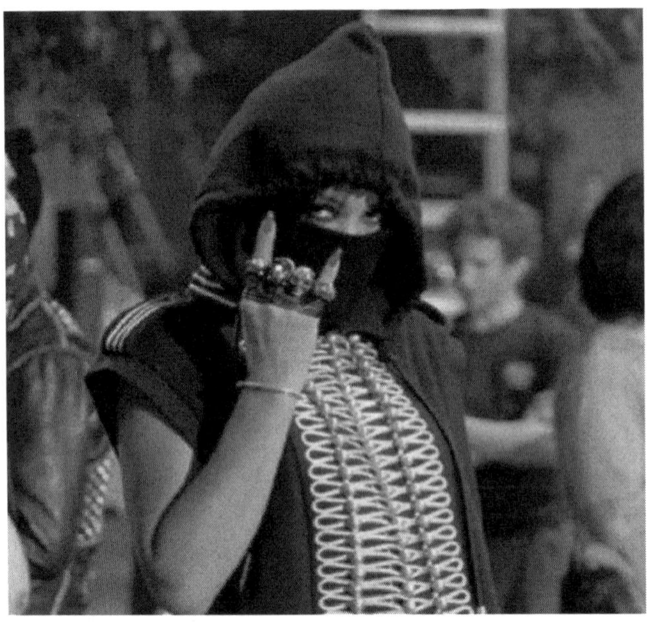

Rock and Heavy-Metal music used to be understood to be satanic music and those who opened themselves up to satanic influence through this media were usually Caucasian young adults. Young blacks, for the most part, steered away from this sort of music and from its overt satanic spin. The perversions used to re-introduce Baal worship and Satanism back into our community were sex (Asherah) and violence (Baal). The Hebrew people have always been easily led astray sexually and that holds true today. The Valkyries have been deployed again and the men that should be sensitive to satanic influences have been reduced to Ahab's spirit. The overt sexual nature of most media today is used to disarm men, while at the same time teaching young women to channel this demon. They are taught to be a "Female" which is not what Eve created as. The concept of being a "Woman" today has nothing to do with what the scriptures say and the world has managed to call what a "Female" was at the beginning, a "Woman". The idea that a woman should be promiscuous, objectionable, unfeminine, unrepentant and detached is masked by the fact that she is naked and easy to get to sexually. In a society of stimulation junkies, the packaging has become more important than the contents as we watch female celebrities who have been in front of our children since infancy, open themselves up to demons. They strip off their clothes and advocate living in a way that no parent would want. They lead our children into gross sexual perversion, rebellion against parents, drug abuse, harmful relationships, diseases and all kinds of other undesirable things, but we pay the cable bill and allow it to be delivered right into our homes. It seems that we haven't learned much from history. Where we find ourselves today is par for the course and only legalized prostitution and public pornography are the things that are left. The truth is that we have already come to this place, just not publicly.

Nothing New Under the Sun.....

The truly disgusting thing about what Jezebel does today is that it ultimately victimizes its host. After this person has demolished the lives of those who would have tried to love them, most folks that understand the destructive nature of that person will remove them from their circles of trust. These people lose close relationships, spouses, children, friends, business associates and ultimately end up alone. The word "Jezebel" literally means "No Cohabitation". The feminine sorcery people under the influence of this demon make use of is deeply dark and satanic. It has caused the destruction of many and is critical to what the enemy is currently doing in the earth right now.

Overt Sexuality and No Regard for Order.... Know your enemy....

Most (I'm guessing about 99.7%) of our sisters today are wrestling with the Jezebel spirit. This spirit is what makes these sisters not fit to cohabitate. Think about the mind that will submit to a man in order to become a wife, then once a wife, become the most putrid example of wife or mate imaginable. That makes no sense at all, but Satan's ultimate goal in going heavily after the minds of women was to counter what the Father intended when He told Israel not to marry wives outside of the nation of Israel. You'd better know that today's thuggish, whorish or gay children were nourished on the milk of possessed women and absence or weakness of diminished men. Today, Jezebel tells a woman to act like a female (Lilith). Once no man will provide for this woman, she makes the government "Daddy" by going on welfare. One strict requirement of the ability to receive public aid is that there can be no man in the home. The government (beast) doesn't care how many men come into the house to defile it, but will go absolutely ballistic is a true man comes into the home to heal it. The children she has are had to feed the state. These possessed women are the source of "Billions" of dollars in state administrative funding AND the prison industry. Children born into poverty are statistically prone to higher rates of incarceration and it is unimaginable how many men are placed into the jail for child support violations. Does the state really care about any of these issues? Not really, but they do care about the money.

For my brothers out there that are in order, if you want to really find out where a woman's mind is on the subject of a "Proper" life for her and your child, tell the woman you want to marry her. You see, a "Female" can't be a wife. A female will take the check and send you to jail, but you put her into a position where she is expected to cook, clean, smile and agree. Let her know that she will need to wash your underwear, fold clothes and submit. My guess is that if you were man enough to make the female have to choose, many men wouldn't be in jail for fleeing or avoiding their child support responsibilities. Why? Because this spirit cannot take a strong man that is rooted in and submitted to the Word of the Most High. Jezebel will flee. Try me on that one..

6. The Attacks of the Jezebel........

As a spirit, Jezebel displays two forms of attack on men, depending on what situation it finds itself in at the time. The most common attack is the feminine or type A attack. But in certain situations, this demon will display overtly male characteristics. This form is called type B.

Think of this picture as a spiritual thermometer... If you want this, pray......

Type A Attack. The Type A attack consists of flatteries and overt sexuality. In this mode, the Jezebel seems to submit and it seems that she is giving the man everything he wants. Understand that a simple minded men can be manipulated and controlled through his penis. Remember, Lilith wanted to have sexual relations in the dominant or controlling position. She has sex like a man. In this form she seduces and uses her femininity to control. On a spiritual level, her sexuality is intended to cause man to defile himself. It seems like you are getting something from her (sex), but all the while, she is draining your spiritual potency and ability to connect with the Holy Spirit. This is why preachers that are active in sexual immorality (or any sin for that matter) should not be preaching to anyone. The first chapter of the Book of Wisdom reads this way:

Wis 1:1 Love righteousness, ye that be judges of the earth: think of the Father with a good (heart,) and in simplicity of heart seek him.

Wis 1:2 For he will be found of them that tempt him not; and sheweth himself unto such as do not distrust him.

Wis 1:3 For froward (rebellious) thoughts separate from Father YHWH: and his power, when it is tried, reproveth the unwise.

Wis 1:4 For into a malicious soul wisdom shall not enter; nor dwell in the body that is subject unto sin.

Wis 1:5 For the holy spirit of discipline will flee deceit, and remove from thoughts that are without understanding, and will not abide when unrighteousness cometh in.

Wis 1:6 For wisdom is a loving spirit; and will not acquit a blasphemer of his words: for Abba is witness of his reins, and a true beholder of his heart, and a hearer of his tongue.

Wis 1:7 For the Spirit of the Most High filleth the world: and that which containeth all things hath knowledge of the voice.

Anonymous (2011-03-30). Deuterocanonical Books of the Bible Apocrypha (Kindle Locations 3904-3912). . Kindle Edition.

So, in this form, the attack is spiritual. It requires a man to violate what should be his first marriage to the Word of our Father. In this way, this attack is more dangerous than the type B attack. This world teaches men when women give it up, it's all good. But, in the spirit, submitting yourself to Jezebel's perversion is just like eating rat poison. The goal here is to weaken and manipulate. This kind of puts a different spin on Beyonce slinking around on the stage and Rihanna "Touching" herself into another light huh? The Jezebel spirit has been deployed to cause men to submit themselves to sin. This is similar to Adam's failure in standing on the Word with Eve.

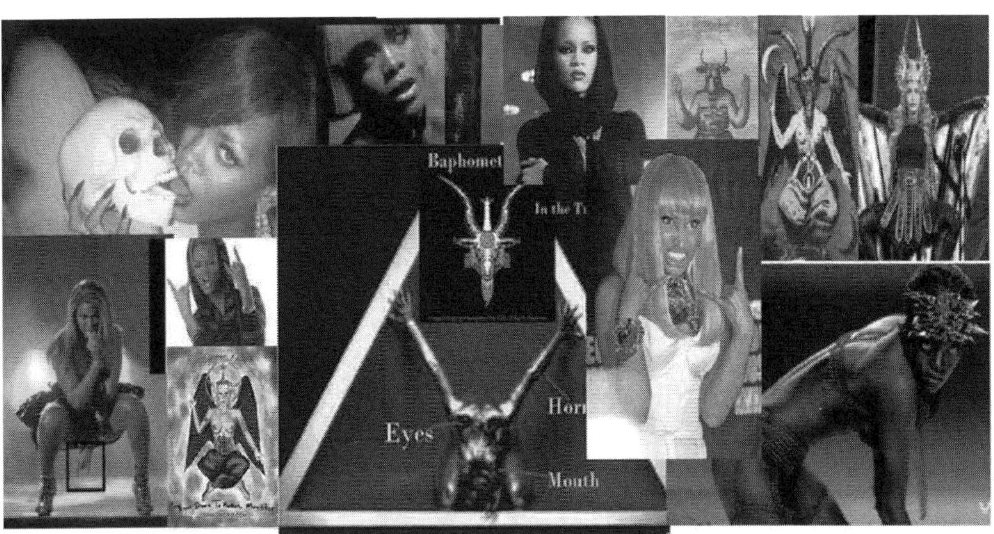

Once this spirit imagines that it has the upper hand, then you will see who this woman serves.

<u>The Type B Attack.</u> The Type B Attack is the masculine side of this spirit. It occurs when the Jezebel spirit feels it has power and authority. In this form, it will mercilessly attempt to destroy or harm its target. In this form, we see the truly Satanic essence of this demon. From this position, it will do or say anything to harm and destroy. It will inflict the most severe form of mental torture possible on its target. It will seek to destroy

anything and everything attached to its target. It will tell the most unbelievable lies with the intent of harming its target. It will, without remorse, destroy this person's whole world along with its own if necessary. Type B attacks are about force and intimidation. These attacks in some cases result in physical violence. Mental torture is the preferred form of torment. From this position, Jezebel causes depression, anguish, anxiousness, paranoia and the like. The intent is to take peace from her victim to the point of surrender or even suicide. Once a man discloses his secrets or allows this demon the upper hand, then its true evil is revealed. The demon will switch back and forth between these two types of attacks, with the goal of invalidating and eventually destroying its victim. We must be sensitive to both types of this demon's witchcraft.

The truly demonic aspect of any woman that would employ these tactics is that they have no concern for themselves, their children, the community or any uninvolved person that is attached to the attack. This is one of the primary indicators that you are dealing with a Jezebel possessed person.

7. Jezebel in the church...

Compromise the word? Expect Rebellion... You all had to know this was coming......

So, what can be said when a female bishop, who knows the word, rationalizes becoming a lesbian and accuses the church of sexual bias? What can be said is that we are coming to the end and scripture is being fulfilled in our sight! We can say "Rejoice", because our Father's word is true. In Detroit, Bishop Allyson D. Nelson Abrams (above) steps down from her position in order to marry another female bishop. <u>They plan on opening a church of their own</u>. What the she-Bishop doesn't understand with this move is that she has followed in the footsteps of the apostate Catholic church. In her fallen state, she thinks that her perspective on the word "Allows" for her behavior, saying that people just don't "Digest" the Word like she does. Where is it written that priests should bugger young boys and take vows of chastity? Where is it written that a religion can take away from or add to the Holy Scriptures? That is what "Religion" has done since Nimrod. This she-Bishop was once married, but it takes "Real" strength to submit. This mindset and rationalization is a product of new age theology and the spirit of Jezebel that is running rampant in the black Christian church.

1 Timothy 2-9:15

9 *In like manner also, that women adorn themselves in modest apparel, with shamefacedness and sobriety; not with broided hair, or gold, or pearls, or costly array;*

10 *But (which becometh women professing godliness) with good works.*

11 *Let the woman learn in silence with all subjection.*

12 *But I suffer not a woman to teach, nor to usurp authority over the man, but to be in silence.*

13 *For Adam was first formed, then Eve.*

14 *And Adam was not deceived, but the woman being deceived was in the transgression.*

15 *Notwithstanding she shall be saved in childbearing, if they continue in faith and charity and holiness with sobriety.*

The construct of the church is being destroyed from the inside out, mainly because as an institution, it tries to cheapen the relevance of the scriptures themselves. A good bit of what you see that is going wrong in the church has everything to do with these verses from 1 Timothy on women teaching and usurping authority over man. The demeanor and apparel suggestions are clearly to set up to lend to an environment where men are not swayed by women and spirits are not allowed destructive access to that device responsible for instructing and leading the assembly. Women did not receive the breath of our Father. Not even in the case of Lilith, did our Father breath into any thing in His creation, besides Adam. So spirits are constantly speaking to the women, trying to gain access through them. If it is not apparent to you at this point, what we call the church and what the scriptures identify as the "Assembly" are two different things. How do I know this? Revelation 2:18-29 is clear that what is allowed in today's "Church" was never meant to be allowed in our Father's assembly. I say that to you because the assembly was supposed to be the place that taught the Word and modeled the people's compliance with the Word. Does your church do that?

Today, most of what has become what we know as the "Church" experience is rooted in the filth of Jezebel. If you noticed in the previous chapters and from the scripture, this spirit loves to be in a position to influence or degrade the worship of the Most High. The "Person" of Jezebel went into what was supposed to be the nation of the Most High and did what? Changed the religious practice. How do I know it is the same spirit as was described above? Queen Semiramis ran the "Religion" of Babylon and then got around to destroying the strongest men near her; her husband and then her son. The church today is structured to undermine the order of the home, by placing the wives of men into positions of authority within its administrative bodies or even in ministry. What you end up getting are women who are broken and full of foul spirits, that the men of the church can't or won't manage. These women end up influencing what is preached, how it is preached or even if certain things are preached at all. You get bitter divorced and single women advising young newlyweds and passing on their opinions based upon their own past relationships. Single female ministers, having children out of wedlock, advising and teaching the younger women or even in some cases, the men also. This spirit is perfectly at home in situations lacking structure and order or a situation where they can challenge the set order.

It would be one thing if those in charge of churches stood against this influence, but it is quite the opposite because the church is designed to allow the spread of this and other demons. These spirits are nurtured by the church which seems to "Need" a body of wayward females in order to operate. This spirit in a group of women ends up with that group seeking out one another within the body and conducting themselves much like a coven of witches (not knowing that the spirit that drives them is a witchcraft spirit). So now, you have women's clichés that run the whole assembly. First you had the "Preacher's Wife". Then you had the "First Lady". Now, you have this notion of the "Co" Pastor, mainly because men are weakened by the spirit of Jezebel. Where can this spirit take the church next except that more scripture will be fulfilled?

Romans 1:24-27:

24 Wherefore Father YHWH also gave them up to uncleanness through the lusts of their own hearts, to dishonour their own bodies between themselves:

25 Who changed the truth of our Father into a lie, and worshipped and served the creature more than the Creator, who is blessed for ever. Let It Be.

26 For this cause the Most High gave them up unto vile affections: for even their women did change the natural use into that which is against nature:

27 And likewise also the men, leaving the natural use of the woman, burned in their lust one toward another; men with men working that which is unseemly, and receiving in themselves that recompence of their error which was meet.

On the flipside of that equation, wounded women are always present in the church with the notion of leading the men astray sexually or otherwise, all the way up to and including the person leading the church. You can generally find Jezebel around the children. This was the main intent of what Paul said to Timothy regarding women in the church. If the suggestion was followed, based upon the fall in the garden, the church of Thyatira would not have received the reprimand that it did from our MessiYah. It read as such:

Revelation 2:18-23

18 And unto the angel of the church in Thyatira write; These things saith the Son of YHWH, who hath his eyes like unto a flame of fire, and his feet are like fine brass;

19 I know thy works, and charity, and service, and faith, and thy patience, and thy works; and the last to be more than the first.

20 Notwithstanding I have a few things against thee, because thou sufferest that woman Jezebel, which calleth herself a prophetess, to teach and to seduce my servants to commit fornication, and to eat things sacrificed unto idols.

[21] And I gave her space to repent of her fornication; and she repented not.

[22] Behold, I will cast her into a bed, and them that commit adultery with her into great tribulation, except they repent of their deeds.

[23] And I will kill her children with death; and all the churches shall know that I am he which searcheth the reins and hearts: and I will give unto every one of you according to your works.

The Major Gospel Fellowship business model has seen huge success in its expansion. Years ago, I attended a conference held in Atlanta and the participation was so large that it filled the entire Georgia Dome, for almost a week. I was able to stay on afterward and meet with other non-affiliated church leaders in the area, as I was working out the mission and purpose of my own ministry. In speaking with those, obviously salty, smaller church leaders, many of them had lost significant numbers to the newly introduced Gospel Fellowship model. What was different? This fellowship model was willing to license women while the others would not. Forget the word or the quality of what was being preached. In order to exploit an exception to the word, women left these other churches in droves.

This spirit "LOVES" the current state of the Christian Church and the weakness of its leaders. The Jezebel spirit is rampant as it seduces leadership, corrupts ministry, poisons women and perverts the thinking of children. Women in the pulpit asserting authority over men has now become women preachers and bishops trading the role of a woman with the ambitions of the female. What is coming to the world with the crash of the world currency and support systems will show these women that they are, in fact, women, who need men. Satan's system of minimizing the importance of a man is quickly coming to an end. The Jezebel spirit has caused many women to forsake their role and the covering of men. The new world will bring life back to the facts of the matter and it will be shown that nothing actually changed.

8. What is really going on with homosexual men?

You can't expect your woman to come home sane after hanging out with the insane all day..

Recently, I Facebook'ed with a sister that attended the last church I attended before embracing the truth. Her post is as follows:

Soap Box Alert: I am so SICK AND TIRED of Christians getting ridiculed for our beliefs. How can you be okay that we're Christians, but if we are asked a question and respond to it according to our belief system we are then treated as judgmental. In actuality, the people who are being judgmental are the people reacting. I just listened to a radio broadcast where two people were essentially bashing my religious beliefs. That is okay right? Because they were talking about Phil Robertson RESPONDING TO A QUESTION about homosexuality? You do NOT have to agree with him but when you begin to mock and undermine Christianity you are doing the same thing you are accusing him of doing! I don't believe some of the preposterous stuff that other people believe, but that is what they believe and it is their right. (And some of it is really stupid). All I'm saying is this, if you don't agree with someone- and you think it's stupid- shake your head and move on.

To which, I answered:

I wish I knew what Dr. Phil said so I could understand the context of what prompted the statement. In general, I beat the crap out of Christianity. Why would I do that after years and years in the church? It has everything to do with the "Scriptures" and how Christianity as a practice, violates what is written in the word. Where this practice puts people in danger is that the MessiYah never came here to invalidate the old testament law...Matthew 5:17.... There is also the issue with what our treatment of sin boils down to. In the baptist practice, we are supposedly forgiven for sin one time at the time that we accept the MessiYah as our savior...then all sin, past, present and future are forgiven... but in the scriptures, when Yahshua gave forgiveness to the prostitutes and reprobates that the Pharisees shook their heads at, he told them "Sin No More". That means that repentance is more than just a shake, fall-out and an I'm sorry. The more I read, the less I can take my former religion. The more I study, the more I see doctrines that don't tie back to the book and then when I read that Satan deceived the "Whole" world, I have to look at who looks more like the "Whole" world and who looks like the remnant? If the MessiYah didn't come here to invalidate the law, then that means that the Most High still considers homosexuality an abomination of an act, unless that sin is truly in the past for that person... ie, they "Repented"....and will sin no more in that way. With animals and fish dying, meteors in the sky, earthquakes causing sink-hole, the oceans filling up with oil(blood) and radiation (wormwood), I'm thinking the book itself is going to hold more weight than a practice and a billion dollar business model.... How many folks do you figure are going to come to a church that preaches straight out the bible with no chasers? That's the main issue that I have with Christianity as a practice and a business. Thanks for the soap box though sis. Most folks just blow by what is being said without understanding any of it.

The main point of the discussion was to illustrate that a modern day church "Cannot" function by preaching our Father's truth, as it is written. Now, this conversation went fairly well with this sister disagreeing and she and I parting, knowing each other's stance. Upon going back into the discussion to show my wife how it had gone, several of the comments showed as "Edited". If you know Facebook, you can go back and edit your responses. It was very obvious that I was no longer talking to the person I started the discussion with. With several points added to each of those already discussed, I began to work back through what was "Added". After my first post, this sister abruptly told me that the discussion was shut down (because about 41 people were now following the discussion). I made reference to the fact that I didn't have a chance to address all of the new points and then shared my scriptural basis for my posts. The first chapter of "The Church Book" or the Wisdom of Sirach. Then after that post, this sister made reference to a very openly homosexual choir leader, who I'd had to address in this forum previously. It was for this discussion particularly that I have had to add a chapter to this book. The conversation had gone very cordially until this "Homosexual" showed up. This sister's attitude changed "Completely" and an opportunity to speak on the scriptures became a shooting match.

In meditating on this interaction, I think back to many in this and other churches; and the spirit made it clear that this was no isolated incident. This is now a norm amongst our sisters in general. We know that the Jezebel spirit reigns in our sisters and especially so in those indoctrinated into the black Christian church. But what is really going on with the homosexual man in relation to what we already know about our sisters? Why are our sisters so quickly influenced by a man who "Hates" his own manhood and true manhood in others? The answer to this question hit me like a ton of bricks. It is because it is the same filthy Jezebel spirit, but in control of a man.

I think it is safe to say that we have lost something, when this can be called "Normal".

What exactly is a Homosexual? He is a man that believes that he is a woman, mistakenly born as a man. He believes this so much that he, as a man, will allow another man to place his penis into his own rectum to the point of ejaculation. The men that engage in this behavior feel as though it is Father YHWH that has done this to them. In this delusion, MANY blaspheme our Father by suggesting that a perfect Creator made a mistake, simply because a person wants a certain type of sin. The truth is that demons and sin have detached these men from reality.

Romans 1:28:

28 And even as they did not like to retain the Father in their knowledge, Abba gave them over to a reprobate mind, to do those things which are not convenient;

29 Being filled with all unrighteousness, fornication, wickedness, covetousness, maliciousness; full of envy, murder, debate, deceit, malignity; whisperers,

30 Backbiters, haters of Father YHWH, despiteful, proud, boasters, inventors of evil things, disobedient to parents,

31 Without understanding, covenantbreakers, without natural affection, implacable, unmerciful:

32 Who knowing the judgment of the Most High, that they which commit such things are worthy of death, not only do the same, but have pleasure in them that do them.

Today, it is not enough for men of these sort to have a right to privacy to do what they want, but "Society" must accept what they do and tell them that their behavior is normal, when it is not. This is classic Satan. I'll qualify this with an example. I am a 300+ pound, dark man. If I decided one day that I was a "Chicken", born in the body of a man AND I decided to go into public and squeeze eggs out of my behind, the authorities would very quickly put me into an insane asylum. But the "Law" in this country, the president and now the pontiff of Rome find nothing insane about the same 300+ pound me, squeezing into a dress, high heals, a wig and make-up, to act as though I am a Female. In general, you can see the tampering of Satan in situations that simply make no sense.

A homosexual man, in this way, is not sane. His delusional behaviors signify this fact. But the truly demonic influence apparent here is the fact that they will seek to force the society at large to validate the behavior. Furthermore, the sin these men engage in opens them up to all types of demonic influences and outright possession. This is what the Jezebel spirit does in general. It destroys men. Our sisters are drawn to this spirit in a man <u>because it is familiar</u>. Take a look at the commonalities.

- Both hate structure and order and work actively to undermine the established rule.
- Both hate the headship that the Father placed in manhood.
- Both gossip.
- Both seek to control and manipulate others.
- Both are loud and obnoxious.
- Both will seek to destroy anything that stand in the way of something they want.
- Both are attracted to power and authority.
- Neither is capable of logical discussion or reasoning.
- Neither will accept being corrected or proved wrong.
- Both engage in coven-like cliques.

- Both are bothered when they hear the words "Submission" or "Righteousness".
- Both will argue against and seek loopholes in the Word of the scripture.

I could go on, but I think you get my point. All of these things are outlined in the life of Jezebel. This demon shows itself in acts of contempt against the scriptures. If a church or pastor did actually stand for the word, you can trust me when I say, they would at the very least, stop tithing. Because of money and even more than that, because of the laws of this land, it is illegal for a church receiving 501c3 tax exemptions to preach the unadulterated truth from Leviticus or Revelation. The Jezebel spirit, because of its nature, would make any institution that does this pay, regardless of whether or not a preacher reads directly from the book.
The ultimate goal of Jezebel's possession of men is to begin to control the environment. Many churches and now governmental bodies are squarely in the control of those who are not sane. State and municipal government bodies and agencies are "Filthy" with homosexuals and pagans. Satan knows the real strength of a man even if he himself doesn't know it. By making a man a "Diva", the Father's breath is misused to promote the Anti-Creation agenda of the end times.

The bottom line here brothers and sisters is that a homosexual man is not channeling a woman's spirit as he thinks. He is channeling the spirit of the "Female" or the spirit of Lilith.

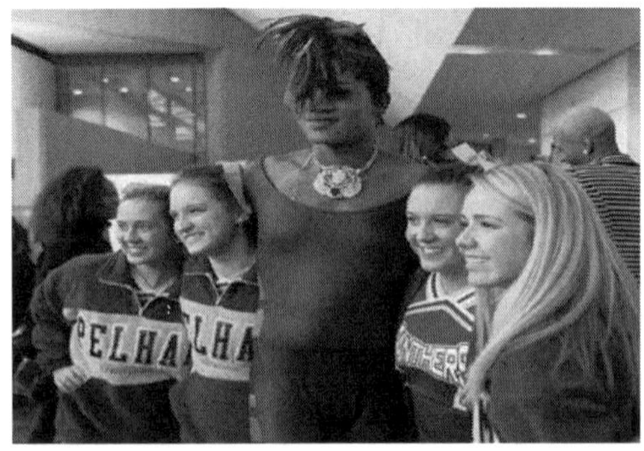

Sorry Kids.... That's not sane......

His rebellion and hatred of the proper order intended for a man give this away, without a doubt. Type A and Type B attack patterns are also characteristic of a man infected with this demon. Know your enemy and that this spirit hides in wayward men just as easily as a woman in these last days. It is sad to me that our sisters are influenced more by broken men than those that would seek to make them wives and mothers. It is sad to me that a woman can't see the illness of mind in hating the role that the Father has given her, in raising His generations of children. The homosexual man will not create life and will guide our sisters into hatred of her place. This is rampant in churches all across the United States and pastors say nothing. In truth, because these men have forsaken the word and the Father, they are alone and facing literal demons in these gay men and pastor simply doesn't have the strength or the ammunition. This is by design and many simply don't care to deal with it. The reckoning will come at the hand of our MessiYah. By His hand and by Fire, this mess will be cleansed. HalleluYah!

9. An Encounter with a Witch.....

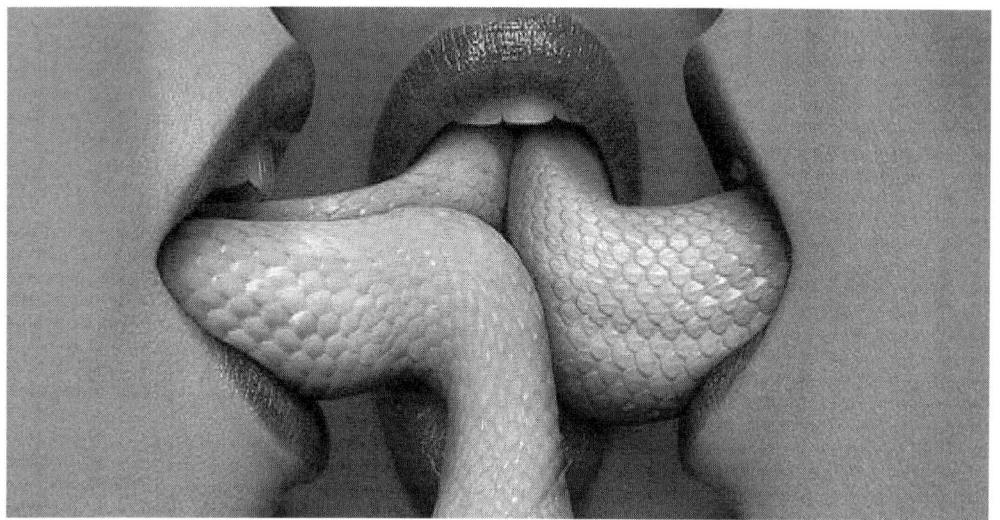

A project like this disrupts and discomforts demons all throughout the aer (the lower atmosphere or Satan's domain). Some of the pre-writing for this book was done in the blogosphere, on hub pages like two years ago. The blog is titled "The Two Spirits of Woman and the Struggle between Them" and is still available for viewing and comments. This blog has really sat for a good while, but when I began writing "Jezebel Rising", I got a comment on the blog from a modern day witch or wiccan or whatever they go by. I think it is a good idea to share this comment here in the book so that people can get a good idea of the depths of the delusion that these women go to once infected with this demon. The "Rationalization" of what is known to be wicked will stun you.

*"**Being** 4 days ago*

You take Scripture as Hagar, or in bondage to letterofword. Being male, you try to take it as literally male and female.

Lilith is the part of a human that others attempt to subjugate. Adam is the part that does the subjugating. Eve is the part that becomes subjugated and bowed. In knowing that it is subjugated it tries to break free to find it's way back to spirit past it's subjugation by Adam. This is where it once again becomes spirit, no longer bound to the will of man (Adam) but fully aware of the will of the Divine . Jezebel and her ilk are not daughters of Lilith. They are daughters of Eve, subjugated by Adam and fighting to get free of it through their own will and not the Divine will they would get from Lilith. None of this had anything to do with actual males and females. Or men and women. It was a way of describing a people, that because of language and the way it takes male and female (ex. Le, La) and assigns those aspects to things, concepts and émotions and not just physical biological gender. It has been misused for eons by MAN, following YAHWEH, in direct defiance of Divine and coming directly from that tree you speak so ill of.

I went looking at the behest of Spirit, having given my will, knowing only when I submitted and quit allowing the writings of man in one book to cause me to seek answers that only satisfied my fear of those words instead of the direct will of All That Is (Divine). You might want to try it. It's an experience I wouldn't trade for anything.

Try being a nerd in several religions and spiritual concepts, being open to the will of Divine, not Yahweh who is only the male aspect and gives you as a person only a distorted view of the human condition, and also in history and psychology. When you continuously ask the feminine to serve the masculine in chains, the female wisdom (Lilith) will run down inside her to the desolate places because she was not created to submit Divine did not ask her to, Yahweh and Adam did. And the man in you will kill her self expression and her ability to find her own path to Divine (those pesky demon child thoughts that make her wonder why you have decided to chain her, subjugate her, religate her to the role of a crude vessel and slave to be used to your whim and to be silent when that is NOT what the Scriptures are telling you to do and cause her to question why she should put up with being less than what she was created for, just your flesh to be used and beaten and cast aside as you see fit, treated worse than your own filth.)

Women with a spirit of Lilith don't need to be Miley. They aren't fighting to recognize themselves and they are already free. And only a very good man could recognize her and what her existence means for your angry, jealous God."

Freaky right? Many of you would think I made this up, but you should go to my blog page and see it for yourself. "http://elderyoungman.hubpages.com/hub/2femalespirits". This was literally a witch, that has give herself over to literal demons and has wrapped her mind around what she calls "Divine". In the first chapter of

"The Corruption and Planned Destruction of YHWH's Creation", we discuss the two falls of man. Both falls are attributable to the "gods" or fallen angels. Wiccans and pagans worship these devils. Even more detached is that they follow a narrative where these fallen beings are actually good and our Father is evil. There was a time when this thought pattern was consider fringe and was practiced in the shadows. Today, this thought pattern has been rebranded and is very much in the majority. You may not know its sound with no chasers as this person laid it out on my blog page, but you probably have heard of Common Core, Lucis Trust and the New Age movement. This mindset of the witch will become progressively more and more mainstream. Before the spirit of Jezebel stripped off her clothes and started twerking, she inhabited influential female scholars. One such scholar is Helena Blavatsky. Her discipline called "Theosophy" was an inverted description of characters of the bible. Blavatsky taught that it was Satan who was actually the MessiYah. In Blavatsky's world, Satan is described as the "Bringer of Light" to humanity. This "Theosophy" is the basis to new age Christianity and the process by which the Word of the Holy Scriptures has been distorted. The "Theosophist" or more plainly put, devil worshipper, seeks to deify Satan and paint his temptation of Eve as the spark of mankind's conscious. They have painted the adversary as a teacher of "Self" consciousness. Another such scholar is the theosophist Alice Bailey. Alice Bailey's work laid the groundwork for many of the philosophies held by the United Nations. Her publishing company, once called "The Lucifer Trust" is now a UN NGO called the Lucis Trust. Now, you might think that all of this is far detached from your world. I once thought this way also, but then you come to understand that these Theosophical ideals have been taught to several generations of elites and their minions, as colleges and school curriculums are influenced by the UN. One such minion is Margaret Sanger, the creator of Planned Parenthood. Most people don't seem to understand that Ms. Sanger was a Nazi and a racist, who ascribed to the occult practice of Eugenics. Yes, Ms. Sanger was a Theosophist....or more clearly stated, a devil worshipper. You can see the Jezebel pattern of conflict in these statistics:

- *Nothing in American claims more lives than abortion, with some 1.2 million children being killed each year.*
- *And the African-American community bears a disproportionate number of these abortions. Although blacks make up 13% of the US population, black women have some 36% of the abortions. A Black baby is 5 times more likely to be killed in the womb than a White Baby.*
- *Some 1,784 African-American children are killed by abortion each day.*
- *Abortion in the African-American community has killed more than has AIDS, cancer, diabetes, heart disease, and violent crime combined.*
- *For every two African American women that get pregnant one will choose to abort.*
- *Some 3,446 Blacks were lynched in the U.S. between 1882 and 1968, That number is surpassed in less than 3 days by abortion.*
- *Every week more African-Americans are killed by abortion than all people killed in the Viet Nam war*
- *Since 1973, abortion has wiped out over 25% of the African-American population.*

Source: http://www.priestsforlife.org/africanamerican/about.htm

These philosophies are embraced by the new age, the new world order, the United Nations and your local church. Ms. Sanger used prominent so-called Black Preachers to forward this Satanic, anti-creation agenda. Ms. Sanger is only one person in millions that have been indoctrinated into the ideals of Satanism under different, educated sounding names.

So, what you see today in the New Age church, public acceptance of satanic doctrine, abortion laws, homosexuality and population control, these all come from the groundwork laid by these "Theosophists". The United Nations has a major role in many different vital areas of life and it is controlled by devil worshippers. The UN is the skeleton of the one world government spoken of in Revelation.

It is a hard thing to get one's mind around, but these people think the exact opposite of what you think. When dealing with them, you must understand that those things that you think are good, they think are abomination. Those things you know are abomination are their ways. They teach these things to their children and they see you and me as unenlightened and not worthy to live into the new age. The spirit of Jezebel is integral to the advancement of Satan's goal. Remember, this spirit, even when it seems to promote the idea of strong femininity, is still subject to the dominion of a male deity. Lilith submitted herself to Eblis and bore demon children. These women who were obsessed with the "Anti-

Creation" agenda of Satan and the fallen angels, still they ascribe to a spiritual "Male".

As I stated earlier, a project of this sort upsets spirits moving about in the atmosphere. Not only was approached by a witch but others in our study group. It's not so much the book, but the times into which the book is to be sent into. Spirits are becoming more and more active as we approach the end. Witches will either more aggressive or will seek to leave the covens as the spirits they serve begin to require more and more from them. The Jezebel spirit has opened them up so that they either have to fully deny or fully accept the demon spirits they have been dealing with.

10. Summary....Killing the spirit of Ahab....

Ahab must die.....

In wrapping up this edition, we have to remember that there is nothing new under the sun (Ecclesiastes 1:9). This "Mystery" Babylon is orders of magnitudes more wicked than the earlier iterations. Aborted children are blood sacrifices to Moloch. Children killed in wars are sacrifices to the fallen angels of war. Jezebel's role is to facilitate the conception of these children by passing "Her" mind off to women as normal. The Jezebel spirit trains "Females"....Tormentors of men and killers of children. All of this is done in "Submission" to her male head, Satan.

Satan, from the beginning, has understood that man's weakness is his woman. Like a woman will do almost anything for the child that comes out of her, man will do some of anything for the rib that came out of him. His most effective attacks on man, prophet, warrior or on the Hebrew Nation itself has come through women.

- He caused Adam to fall, by tempting Eve.
- Semiramis (Nimrod's wife) set up the Babylonian Mystery Religion (Baal and Asherah worship) and had her husband killed when he threatened her power.
- Semiramis attempted to kill her own son when he grew to manhood.
- Potifar's wife was denied what she wanted and sought to kill Yohseph (Joseph) with a lie.
- Moshe's wife was able to cause him not to circumcise his son, which almost cost him his life.
- Job's wife when he lost everything, tried to turn him against our Father.
- Delilah was able to manipulate Samson into telling his secrets.
- Yohannon (John) the Baptist was set up by Herodias.

These are all indicative of the same rebellious, filthy spirit. These were daughters of Lilith and Jezebel is her namesake. This writing would not be complete without addressing the spirit that Jezebel thrives on. In each case mentioned above, an Ahab spirit was required. What is the Ahab spirit? Like the Lilith demon originated in the garden, the spirit that shaped Ahab's inability to deal with Jezebel, started with Adam. The fall of man "Did NOT" happen when Eve ate of the forbidden fruit. The fall of man happened when Adam ate of the fruit. You have to remember brothers, our Father never breathed into Lilith and He never breathed into Eve. Nothing in the creation, woman, female or angel (or gentile for that matter), EVER received our Father's breath. This whole world was given to Adam. So disobedience to our Father is what caused man to fall in the first place. By repeating this act, we relinquish our authority and walk in the same disobedience. The very first order of business with Ahab is that he never should have married Jezebel. Hebrew Israelite men were "Never" supposed to marry outside of the nation to begin with. This was more-so the case for a King of Israel. The kingdom was degraded from the inside through the bedroom, beginning with the foreign wives of David and Solomon. Abalom's mother Maachah was the daughter of the King of Geshur. Geshur was near Bashan and was known to have been inhabited by the Nephilim. The Israelites were to drive out all of the inhabitants of this land, but did not. Absalom was raised by a woman who was intimately exposed to the heathen worship of the Nephilim. Solomon also had many wives. His son Rehoboam was raised by an Ammonite mother whose name was Naamah. The rebellion of Israel's royalty cost the kingdom. Next, Ahab allowed himself to be separated from his Father, YHWH Most High. Jezebel caused the worship in the whole northern kingdom to change. Ahab knew the order and the law and he forsook both. Ahab was wicked in his own pattern of behavior, in how he dealt with the issue of the vineyard he wanted. Finally, Ahab simply did not attempt to lead Jezebel. She led him. It would seem that the Jezebel spirit does not intend to submit to a strong male head, but that is where you would be mistaken. Jezebel server Baal. The devil is her strong male headship as was the case with Lilith. So, the question of "How" do many of these women do such evil things is answered in two-part harmony.

1. Her male headship is destroyed or weakened.
2. She submits herself to rebellion and sin, which belong to Satan.

So what really happened to our sisters? Hebrew Israelite men and women must understand that this is a little deeper than just a lapse in judgment on the parts of our sisters. This people, us, Negros, are under our Father's curse. This is the Father's will for those that don't seek him out. If we don't seek out our Father, then the curse remains in full effect. Deuteronomy 28:

> 49 *The MOST HIGH shall bring a nation against thee from far, from the end of the earth, as swift as the eagle flieth; a nation whose tongue thou shalt not understand;*
>
> 50 *A nation of fierce countenance, which shall not regard the person of the old, nor shew favour to the young:*

[51] *And he shall eat the fruit of thy cattle, and the fruit of thy land, until thou be destroyed: which also shall not leave thee either corn, wine, or oil, or the increase of thy kine, or flocks of thy sheep, until he have destroyed thee.*

[52] *And he shall besiege thee in all thy gates, until thy high and fenced walls come down, wherein thou trustedst, throughout all thy land: and he shall besiege thee in all thy gates throughout all thy land, which the LORD thy God hath given thee.*

[53] *And thou shalt eat the fruit of thine own body, the flesh of thy sons and of thy daughters, which the LORD thy God hath given thee, in the siege, and in the straitness, wherewith thine enemies shall distress thee:*

[54] *So that the man that is tender among you, and very delicate, his eye shall be evil toward his brother, and toward the wife of his bosom, and toward the remnant of his children which he shall leave:*

[55] *So that he will not give to any of them of the flesh of his children whom he shall eat: because he hath nothing left him in the siege, and in the straitness, wherewith thine enemies shall distress thee in all thy gates.*

[56] *The tender and delicate woman among you, which would not adventure to set the sole of her foot upon the ground for delicateness and tenderness, her eye shall be evil toward the husband of her bosom, and toward her son, and toward her daughter,*

[57] *And toward her young one that cometh out from between her feet, and toward her children which she shall bear: for she shall eat them for want of all things secretly in the siege and straitness, wherewith thine enemy shall distress thee in thy gates.*

[58] *If thou wilt not observe to do all the words of this law that are written in this book, that thou mayest fear this glorious and fearful name, THE LORD THY GOD;*

[59] *Then the LORD will make thy plagues wonderful, and the plagues of thy seed, even great plagues, and of long continuance, and sore sicknesses, and of long continuance.*

This is the loss of our minds and our souls. This is the loss of the mother and the wife as described as a "Woman so Tender". Her covering, the men, are destroyed. This leaves the woman uncovered. What we learn from the Gospels is that our MessiYah returned to the land and found all of the women full of demons. It is no different today. The Willie Lynch method of subjugation causes extreme trauma to a woman. She then loses faith in and denies her headship, which opens her up for demonic possession.

The Ahab spirit is not just weakness brothers, it is rebellion against our Father's order. So the question remains, "What should I do if my woman is possessed by Jezebel's spirit" (and most of them are)? The first thing to do is to right your relationship with your Father. Doing battle with this demon will require the Word. Submit yourself to the Word and then present the order outlined in the Word as the way that you will live. Assert the Father's order and lead. This will present the woman a choice. Either she will open herself to the Word and submit to the place ordained for women in the scriptures or she will rebel and go the way of the Female.

Wisdom of Sirach 25:

Sir 25:13 [Give me] any plague, but the plague of the heart: and any wickedness, but the wickedness of a woman:

Sir 25:14 And any affliction, but the affliction from them that hate me: and any revenge, but the revenge of enemies.

Sir 25:15 There is no head above the head of a serpent; and there is no wrath above the wrath of an enemy.

Sir 25:16 I had rather dwell with a lion and a dragon, than to keep house with a wicked woman.

Sir 25:17 The wickedness of a woman changeth her face, and darkeneth her countenance like sackcloth.

Sir 25:18 Her husband shall sit among his neighbours; and when he heareth it shall sigh bitterly.

Sir 25:19 All wickedness is but little to the wickedness of a woman: let the portion of a sinner fall upon her.
Sir 25:20 As the climbing up a sandy way is to the feet of the aged, so is a wife full of words to a quiet man.
Sir 25:21 Stumble not at the beauty of a woman, and desire her not for pleasure.
Sir 25:22 A woman, if she maintain her husband, is full of anger, impudence, and much reproach.
Sir 25:23 A wicked woman abateth the courage, maketh an heavy countenance and a wounded heart: a woman that will not comfort her husband in distress maketh weak hands and feeble knees.
Sir 25:24 Of the woman came the beginning of sin, and through her we all die.
Sir 25:25 Give the water no passage; neither a wicked woman liberty to gad abroad.
Sir 25:26 If she go not as thou wouldest have her, cut her off from thy flesh, and give her a bill of divorce, and let her go.
Anonymous (2011-03-30). Deuterocanonical Books of the Bible Apocrypha (Kindle Locations 4910-4914). . Kindle Edition.

A Jezebel/Lilith possessed person is a person that hates order and sacrifices children. Whenever you see a woman flip out and murder or maim a child, specifically a male child, this demon is involved. But the sacrifice part is done more subtly in today's culture. Today, that sacrifice is taking a child to daycare and not being a mother, for money. I know that there are many single mothers that don't have a choice in this matter and love their children very much. But what about the ones that do have a choice and choose the career over the child? What about those who wants the status available to a women who will trade submission in the home to submission in the boardroom? Unsubmission and a deep hatred for the proper order are indicative of this demon's influence.

I've known men whose wives have used scripture to tell a man that he "Can't" divorce her. Sirach was once a part of the bible cannon and I can tell you, Jezebel does not like chapters 25 or 26. In either case whether she submits or she rebels, YOU MUST LEAD.... Period. This is something that Ahab would not do. Let King Jehu be your example in how you deal with the Jezebel spirit. Give it no quarter, because it drives those infected with it to insanity. It employs the deepest, darkest Satanism imaginable (and unimaginable) to destroy men. Understand this and move accordingly.

Hear the prayer of a "Woman" and a "Wife"......

1st Book of Adam and Eve-Chapter 5

1 Then Adam and Eve entered the cave, and stood praying, in their own tongue, unknown to us, but which they knew well.

2 And as they prayed, Adam raised his eyes and saw the rock and the roof of the cave that covered him overhead. This prevented him from seeing either heaven or the Father's creatures. So he cried and beat his chest hard, until he dropped, and was as dead.

3 And Eve sat crying; for she believed he was dead.

4 Then she got up, spread her hands toward the Most High, appealing to Him for mercy and pity, and said, "O Father, forgive me my sin, the sin which I committed, and don't remember it against me.

5 For I alone caused Your servant to fall from the garden into this condemned land; from light into this darkness; and from the house of joy into this prison.

6 O Father, look at this Your servant fallen in this manner, and bring him back to life, that he may cry and repent of his transgression which he committed through me.

7 Don't take away his soul right now; but let him live that he may stand after the measure of his repentance, and do Your will, as before his death.

8 But if You do not bring him back to life, then, O Abba, take away my own soul, that I be like him, and leave me not in this dungeon, one and alone; for I could not stand alone in this world, but with him only.

9 For You, O Father, caused him to fall asleep, and took a bone from his side, and restored the flesh in the place of it, by Your divine power.

10 And You took me, the bone, and make me a woman, bright like him, with heart, reason, and speech; and in flesh, like to his own; and You made me after the likeness of his looks, by Your mercy and power.

11 O Father YHWH, I and he are one, and You, O Father, are our Creator, You are He who made us both in one day.

12 Therefore, O Father YHWH, give him life, that he may be with me in this strange land, while we live in it on account of our transgression.

13 But if You will not give him life, then take me, even me, like him; that we both may die the same day."

14 And Eve cried bitterly, and fell on our father Adam; from her great sorrow.

I think it is safe to say that Eve learned the difference between herself and the "Female". This is the prayer of a wife and help-meet. Make a note.

Finally, my brothers and sisters, pray. Live your life according to the scriptures and the commandments. Make this a requirement for anyone that you let into your circle of trust and you will reduce the risks of coming into contact with a Jezebel possessed person. Submission to the Word will ultimately protect you. Be of good cheer... Be courageous and do not remain silent when Jezebel rises in your circles. This spirit is rampant and will remain that way until our Brother MessiYah splits the sky. It will be at that time that women will be broken from acting like females. It will also be at that time that many men who have enabled Jezebel will die. This is all recorded in Isaiah 4th chapter.

Thank you again for your support of YHWH's Light!

Elderyoungman.

Follow us on the web!

Website: www.YHWHsLight.com

Study Media: media.yhwhslight.com

Facebook: https://www.facebook.com/freedomthruscripture

Twitter: www.twitter.com/elderyoungman

YouTube: www.youtube.com/elderyoungman

Blog: www.hubpages.com/elderyoungman

Credits and Thank you's:

Yahya Bandele – COFAH Network.

Ramont Coleman-- K.O.H.I.A.H (Kingdom of Heaven Is At Hand)

Chike Akua – Imani Enterprises.

Rev. Glenn Dennard – Family of Faith Ministries

Rev. John Haddix – Macadonia Baptist Church

Mrs. Yelisa S. Williams – YHWH's Light

Ms. Marjorie Renfro – YHWH's Light

Available on CreateSpace and Amazon.com

	**The Corruption and Planned Destruction of YHWH's Creation.** The way you find the world today is no accident. Many books outlining what you see today were removed from your bible. Let's take a look at the history of this world from the full context of the "Missing" scriptures and you will see. What has happened in the world is no deep dark mystery but is based in the same rebellion witnessed in the garden.
	**Recessionproof:Remembrance.** Do you remember how your felt in 2008-2009? Do you feel the same now? Personally, I'm a different person than I was then and I now know more about the political system than I cared to. Remembrance is a walk back through 2009, a word on our present and a prayer for our future.
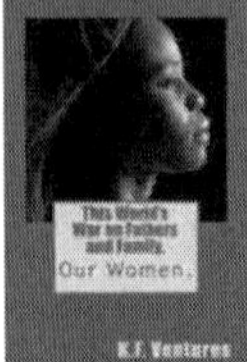	**This World's War on Fathers and Family. Vol. 1-Our Women** Fathers, the epitome of manhood, are at war with this world. This series looks at this war from different angles and based on who is fighting against the father. Volume one deals with the person closest to us, Our Women. Understand your mission as a father and a man better. Understand what she's fighting through also. You may be surprised.
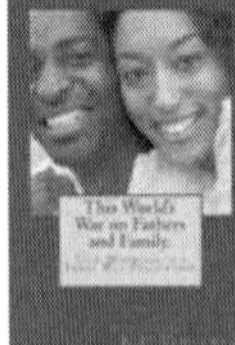	**This World's War on Fathers and Family. Vol. 2-Your Marriage is a 3-Way Fellowship** Volume 2 takes a look at our marriages today. The deception in the garden does not stop with the woman and the man, but also seeks to infect the Father's most sacred union! As believers, we must be diligent in our efforts to maintain healthy marriages because we are the role model for godly relationships. Know your enemy!
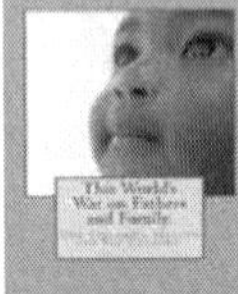	**This World's War on Fathers and Family. Vol. 3-Our Children, Health and Pop Culture.** Volume 3 deals with our children and how this world, through suggestion, chips away at a child's system of values and sanity. Many things are going on and passed off as "Normal". As parents, we must confront this suggestion and protect our children's spirits.
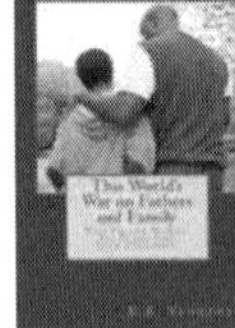	**This World's War on Fathers and Family. Vol. 4-This Fallen World, Its Plans and Your Children.** Have you ever read the 13th amendment to the constitution? If you have, you should know that the exception is more powerful than the rule. There is a billion industry built exclusively on the destruction of our children. The odds are against those who expect sanity from the system.

We offer seminars on this material! Contact Us.

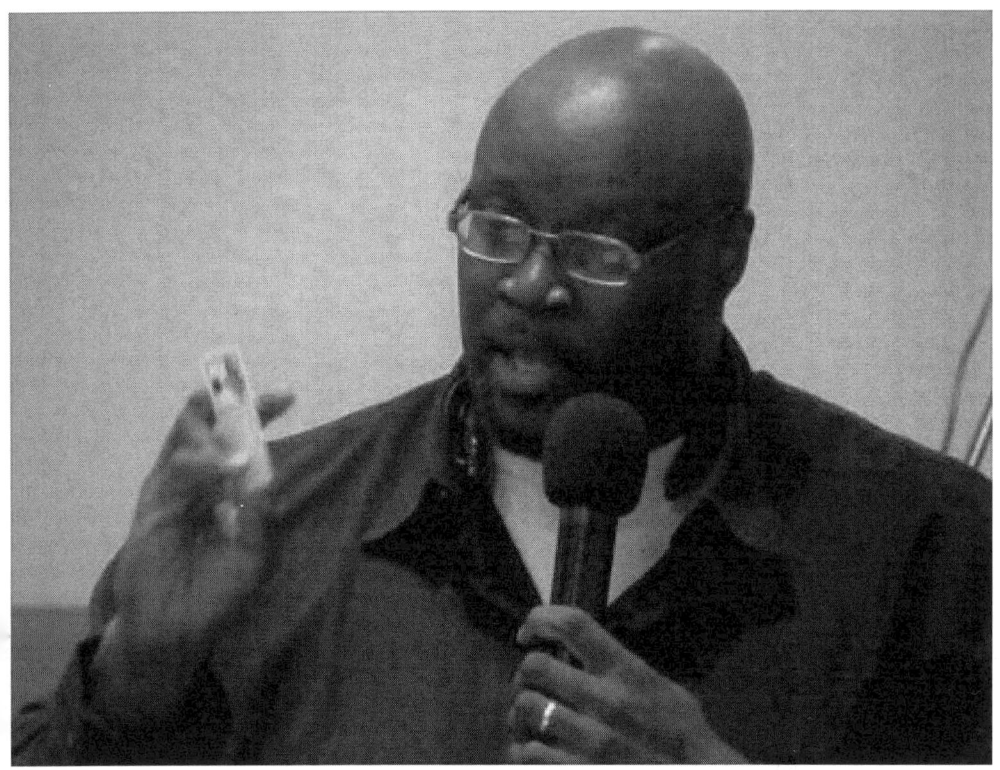

D.L. Williams Consulting and Training
E-Mail: contactus@dlwilliamsconsulting.com
Phone: 1-888-857-8365

Be blessed!

Brother D.L. Williams
YHWH's Light Ministries

Sources:

Brother Yahya Bandele-COFAH Network: Multiple Teachings.

Brother Ramont Coleman-KOHIAH: Multiple Teachings

Anonymous (2011-03-30). Deuterocanonical Books of the Bible Apocrypha (Kindle Locations 4918-4919). . Kindle Edition.

Johnson, Ken (2012-06-12). Ancient Paganism (p. 45). Biblefacts.org. Kindle Edition.

The Fuel Project-Know Your Enemy: Youtube.com

Bringing the Truth Ministries-Discerning the Jezebel Spirit parts 1-4: Youtube.com

The Bible, King James, Cambridge Edition.

The 1st and 2nd Books of Adam and Eve

Made in the USA
Middletown, DE
01 March 2015